The Jiu-Jitsu Way

THADEU VIEIRA

Copyright © 2014 Thadeu Vieira

All rights reserved.

ISBN: 1484853474
ISBN-13: 978-1484853474

DEDICATION

This book is gratefully dedicated to my children.

The love I have for them mysteriously drives my life, seeking enlightenment that hopefully will be radiated to them during our journey.

CAIO, at thirteen;

BENJAMIN, at seven;

RAQUEL, at one.

With love,

Dad.

FOREWORD

Jiu Jitsu is a titanic connection with our ancient carnal forces of being human. It is a thrilling, fast paced, enlivening practice that not only makes our bodies extremely healthy, but perhaps more importantly, strengthens us psychologically, through deep human connection, brought about by vulnerability and reliance on others.

In The Brazilian Jiu Jitsu Way, third degree Jiu Jitsu black belt Thadeu Vieira masterfully provides us with a unique performance guide to high level competitive Jiu Jitsu, a handbook cultivated from a life spent developing champion competitors. He blends his life experience with current psychological research and has created a rare synthesis of performance insight. What you hold in your hands is a gem full of competition and training wisdom. Professor Vieira weaves his teachings with the ancient wisdom of Sun Tzu and Miyamoto Musashi, providing a reflective text of golden lessons that will enhance your connection to the sport. As a psychiatrist and researcher of human athletic performance, I am invigorated by this integration of performance wisdom and ancient Japanese combat philosophy, further informing us of the fruits of the Brazilian Jiu Jitsu.

The vital importance of Jiu Jitsu is that for many of us it becomes a way of life. In my opinion, the reasons for this are that it is a sport of physical connection to others (training partners, audience, referee, coaches), and because of human vulnerability. As researcher and New York Times bestselling author Brené Brown discovered in her extensive research on human connection, the key to maximizing connection to other humans is to become vulnerable and take risks in our relationships. Jiu Jitsu provides healthy vulnerability and risk taking because of the interdependence of the practitioners while sparring, the potential of ceding a submission in front of an audience or a training room, and the reliance on the master for wise individual development. Partners rely on each other for safe training in this submission sport. Even an advanced belt is vulnerable with the ballistic momentum of a larger beginner white belt. There is a connection of touch and emotion, and there is a playful, thoughtful spontaneity in the flowing changing movement of Jiu Jitsu. Vulnerability is woven throughout the fabric of this art.

Vulnerability and risk at their core can be very fun, free spirited, and exploratory. As children, during the happiest times in our lives, we are involved frequently in free play and exploration. Jiu Jitsu epitomizes playfulness in sparring, and it does so while physically making us stronger and more fit, burning calories, lowering cholesterol, maximizing cardiac function, and increasing parasympathetic tone (which is synonymous with relaxation). As a medical doctor and part of a medical community facing epidemics of obesity, chronic stress, cardiovascular disease and diabetes, I recognize Jiu Jitsu's many gifts in battling these community ills. Remarkably, the ultimate benefits of practicing Jiu Jitsu are relaxation, vulnerability and human connection, healthy and mindful eating in order to fuel the body for training, and thoughtful living. Jiu Jitsu supports humility and healthy psychological development, because after all, there is nothing more honest and humbling than entering a training room knowing that there is someone there that will prove on that very day that they are more skilled than you. On the occasions when you are the most talented person in the training room, you've likely built the humility to become a nurturing leader in the sport, as most of the greatest leaders in Jiu Jitsu are. Thus, the allure, the healthy addiction to Jiu Jitsu that so many of us speak of, the all encompassing informing of our minds, muscles, attitudes, dispositions, families.

One of the wonderful expressions of Jiu Jitsu is competitive sport Jiu Jitsu, where all of these factors converge: healthy training, vulnerability, passion, and play. Professor Vieira has masterfully produced a book of high level competition wisdom, gifting us with his detailed reflections on improving Brazilian Jiu Jitsu performance and deepening our connection to the sport. He guides us past inner hurdles in order to cultivate personal victory. In this, we touch not only the ancient combat philosophers, but also our deepest selves and connection to others.

Lucas A Trautman, MD, MPH

September 2014

THADEU VIEIRA

CONTENTS

	Foreword	v
	Preface	xi
	Introduction	Pg 1
1	Drive	Pg 5
2	Readiness	Pg 9
3	Adversary	Pg 13
4	Score	Pg 17
5	Grips	Pg 21
6	Pathway	Pg 27
7	Ambush	Pg 31
8	Assault	Pg 35
9	Opportunity	Pg 39
10	Heart	Pg 43

PREFACE

During the last year I have been asked many times if I would write another book in the same format of the structured journal I published in 2010, The BJJ Notebook. I have received only positive feedback in regards to The BJJ Notebook, and many people have been asking me what comes next. "What comes after, when the journal is complete?" "Could be a similar journal for advanced stages in the Jiu-Jitsu journey?"

I always answer that The BJJ Notebook was conceived to facilitate the learning process of a beginner student. The beginning of the book is full of ideas that are an introduction of the Jiu-Jitsu world. With the engagement of the student in writing, exercising and studying his own journal, the journal contributes to the student by helping to keep he or she motivated and linked to Jiu-Jitsu. As the student commits more and more to this learning activity, the resulting knowledge not only benefits the student, but also the instructor and the whole Jiu-Jitsu movement.

I believe there could be variations and a few additions to The BJJ Notebook, but in the end I think these edits would be redundant. I would rather like to see the student organizing his ideas, perhaps repeating a journal or two, until a certain advanced stage of development is reached.

To go beyond The BJJ Notebook, I would have to breakthrough towards a completely different direction than the journal took, in terms of introducing and guiding a beginner student. Such concepts would encompass high level competitive Jiu-Jitsu. Why high level? Because I believe the sport has been growing and professionalizing in an incredibly positive way, so anything different than that, from self-defense training or recreation, to the competitive Jiu-Jitsu in the amateur level (that in my understanding is a form of recreation as well), are fulfilled previously in The BJJ Notebook.

I have taught students that achieved great results in every important tournament out there. I have developed students who obtained gold medals, for instance, in the Rio de Janeiro State Championship, Brazilian Nationals, Pan American and World Championship. Every single one of these students came to my dojo not knowing how to fall or how to do a front roll and yet, they became victorious in their journey, from scratch. This advent is the purest fulfillment an instructor and student can have in their careers. It is important to always look back and remember the details of the process that lead to such great results. Why are very few able to reach the top and the majority will never make it? There is no general recipe to follow in order to build a champion.

A champion is built from the inside out and not like we say in Brazil - by osmosis. An individual can hang out with world champions, be a disciple of the best in the world and yet, none of that will make one a replica of another.

THE BRAZILIAN JIU-JITSU WAY

*"Aspire to be like Mt. Fuji, with such a broad and solid foundation that the strongest earthquake cannot move you, and so tall that the greatest enterprises of common men seem insignificant from your lofty perspective.
With your mind as high as Mt. Fuji you can see all things clearly.
And you can see all the forces that shape events; not just the things happening near to you."*

- Miyamoto Musashi

THE BRAZILIAN JIU-JITSU WAY

INTRODUCTION

During my near twenty years of practicing Brazilian Jiu-Jitsu, many years were spent teaching, as I pursued the instructorship since the beginning of my blue belt time. It was always rewarding seeing a student that was able to effectively learn something out of a lesson. It was also frustrating seeing students leaving the class without performing or assimilating the teachings like the others.

In a group class set, an instructor shows a position and it is up to the student to "grab" it. Some individuals have different skill levels and for that reason, some will learn faster than others. It is also true that the instructor's teaching methodology and skill in terms of "delivering" is an important role in this process. Some instructors can get frustrated with the students and blame them for not learning and vice-versa. In truth, both parties have to take responsibility to do the best in their roles. The instructor has to do his best to teach and the student has to do the best to study and effectively learn.

Jiu-Jitsu is learned in two methods: theory and practice. Usually teaching and learning by practice is well achieved by instructors and students. The instructor demonstrates and student imitates. The theory behind the learning process is the most neglected part by instructors and students.

Many things in Jiu-Jitsu are not well taught by practicing, for instance the mental strength one must build and maintain during his career in this sport. Strategy, tactics, and the necessity to study an opponent are among many other aspects of learning theory.

The biggest challenge of a successful instructor is to have the intellect and the ability to construct effective theories and transmit it to the students. Another challenge is to come back to such principles and deliver them again over and over to the group throughout the years.

Many great lessons of impact happen only once and are never revisited by the instructor and consequently, the student. If a student misses a day of training where the instructor is inspired and gives one of the best lessons or tips in form of theory – the missing link of many important things can never be found by such student.

The same reasoning goes for the student. Discipline, focus, mental strength, confidence, strategy and others, are elements that must be thoroughly investigated by anyone that wishes to succeed as a competitor in Brazilian Jiu-Jitsu. The competitor must process, build, maintain, adapt, change and execute his skill in the shape of his game, first in theory and later in practice or vice-versa. It is the student's role to bring to himself the responsibility to understand, and to value and to develop such elements.

The purpose of this piece is to gather important lessons I learned and taught throughout my Jiu-Jitsu journey, as essential tools to be revisited, in the hope to help all practitioners out there that have the drive to pursue great results in a high level set of competition.

At last, it is known to many martial artists the following notable books that form the spinal cord of martial arts: The Book of Five Rings and The Art of War. I selected references from these teachings that we all can relate to in a practical way, and I wish you can revisit them quickly by remembering the magnificent quotes of Sun Tzu and Miyamoto Musashi when applied to Brazilian Jiu-Jitsu.

"There is nothing outside of yourself that can ever enable you to get better, stronger, richer, quicker, or smarter. Everything is within. Everything exists. Seek nothing outside of yourself."

- Miyamoto Musashi

1 – DRIVE

Sometimes in training and competitions, students arrive at a point at which it is no longer fun. It starts when it gets tiring, painful, and tedious. This feeling of boredom is the threshold at which it really counts. This is what separates successful athletes from those who don't achieve their goals. Many athletes when they reach this point either ease up or give up because it's just too darned hard. But truly motivated athletes reach this threshold and keep on going.

How many people in your martial arts school would raise their hand if asked who has the goal to be the best of the world in Jiu-Jitsu? Certainly a lot of people would raise their hands. Then reflect with them about how many are doing everything they can to achieve their goals. Only one or two tentative hands go up, maybe none. There is often a big gap between the goals athletes have and the effort they are putting into those goals. It's easy to say that you want to be a successful athlete. It is much more difficult to actually make it happen. If you have this kind of disconnect, you have two choices. You can either lower your goals to match your effort, or you can raise your effort to match your goals. There is no right answer. But if you're truly motivated to be successful, you better make sure you're doing the work necessary to achieve your goals.

There are several signs of low motivation as lack of desire to practice as much as one should: Less than 100% effort in training, missing classes, arriving late or leaving earlier, effort that is inconsistent with your goals.

To have an outstanding drive it means putting 100%

of your time, effort, energy, and focus into all aspects of your Jiu-Jitsu career. It involves doing everything possible to become the best athlete you can be.

Dr. Jim Taylor, specialist in sports psychology claims that motivation for high level athletes begins with what he calls the three D's.

One must find Direction. Before you can attain proper motivation, you must first consider the different directions you can go in competitive Jiu-Jitsu. You have three choices: stop competing completely, continue at your current level, or strive to be the best athlete you can be.

Then comes Decision. With these three choices of direction, you must select one direction in which to go. None of these directions are necessarily right or wrong, better or worse, they're simply your options. Your choice will dictate the amount of time and effort you will put into your journey and how good an athlete you will ultimately become.

At last comes Dedication. Once you've made your decision, you must dedicate yourself to it. If your decision is to become the best athlete you can be, then this last step, dedication, will determine whether you have the drive. Your decision to be your best and your dedication to your career must be a top priority. Only by being completely dedicated to your direction and decision will you ensure that you have proper motivation.

THE BRAZILIAN JIU-JITSU WAY

義

*"Victorious warriors win first and
then go to war,
while defeated warriors go to war first
and then seek to win."*

- Sun Tzu

2 – READINESS

I often use the word "participation" to describe athletes that are not in the highest capacity of mental and physical performance for world class competition. In every tournament division, mainly in the lowest ranks and fewer in the black belt division, there are several competitors that have no chance to win. They may think they have a chance, but they are there to "participate" in normal circumstances.

When beginning a competition career, one must decide as early as possible if the goal of this journey is to win or simply to participate. If participation is the goal, have fun, don't fall into false illusions that you are there to win, and enjoy yourself. This way you can avoid becoming frustrated. If the decision is to become a winner in competition, the athlete must take responsibility and commit himself to all aspects of training that involve a high level of preparation from the inside out.

Sport and Performance Psychologists Dr. David Fletcher and Mustafa Sarkar at Loughborough University determined in a recent study that the world's best athletes shared a unique mental resilience characterized by five key psychological attributes:

A positive personality: Champions possess positive personality characteristics including openness to new experiences, conscientiousness, competitiveness, optimism and proactivity.

Motivation: Gold medalists have multiple internal (i.e. passion for the sport) and external (i.e. proving their worth) motives for competing at the highest level.

Champions consciously judge external pressures as important and so choose to perform in challenging sports environments.

Confidence: Gained from various sources including multifaceted preparation, experience, self-awareness, visualization, coaching, and team mates.

Focus: Champions are able to focus on themselves without distraction, and to concentrate on the process rather than the outcome of events.

Perceived social support: Gold medalists believe high quality social support is available to them, including from family, coaches, team mates and support staff.

The reason why one wants to become a champion is not of such great importance, as many people would think otherwise. It can be for money, for glory, to honor one's family or many other reasons, but in truth none of them matter, none of these reasons will facilitate or diminish the athlete's chances for success. What really matters is how well prepared one will be and how disciplined the student will be in order to maintain the necessary training regiment and the necessary adjustments that this lifestyle will entail. It all begins with mental strength, and perseverance is paramount.

When climbing up the ranks and enrolling in high level adult competition, an athlete should never enter a tournament where the target goals of the season's master plan haven't been met. The coach will establish several targets or benchmarks to guide the athlete's competitive season. Some examples of these targets are: the ideal weight, body fat percentage, nutrition, rest, conditioning exercises regiment, fundamentals training, technique improvement, tactical drills, sparring length, intensity and selection of training partners, strategy research of potential adversaries and practice of adversary's notable skills, the development of forms of neutralization and counters. These, among many others, are aspects that should be part of a season's master plan build up to competition, based in micro and macro goals.

Most of the individuals that believe they are capable of winning and never achieve that result is because they sabotage themselves along the way by not having a master plan or by not having the motivation to execute it. The athletes who strictly live by the above-referenced standards and are driven by <u>habit</u>, rather than will power, will certainly succeed in their careers as they will be ready – equally or better prepared - to face any opponent or adversity in competition.

*"If you know the enemy and know yourself, you need not fear the result of a hundred battles.
If you know yourself but not the enemy, for every victory gained you will also suffer a defeat.
If you know neither the enemy nor yourself, you will succumb in every battle."*

*"To know your enemy,
you must become your enemy."*

- Sun Tzu

3 – ADVERSARY

In modern competitive Jiu-Jitsu it is crucial that one study his adversaries before a tournament. To enter a match with a high chance of success includes knowing beforehand who you're going to fight, what style will you be facing, and what strategies you should enforce in order to neutralize and defeat your opponents.

This type of analysis should begin during the early stages of your Jiu-Jitsu career. We have seen black belts that have been dueling since they were yellow belt kids. In the adult division starting at blue and purple belt it is a certainty that the top four places in the major tournaments will be the same adversaries in the brown and black belt divisions in the future. It is worth looking into, analyzing and profiling each main potential opponent you will be facing in your weight division in all of the four above-referenced ranks.

There is no gambling in competitive Jiu-Jitsu. This art is like an exact science and only with correct study and perseverance one can effectively overcome the obstacles that will be encountered, in order to enter the restricted club of world champions.

Do not assume you can be ready for anyone without thoroughly studying every single possible style you will be encountering. A successful strategist never allow surprises in the middle of combat. If you are not prepared for your opponent and allow yourself to be caught with unexpected moves, you will be gambling with your career.

A serious training program involve the rehearsal of

the styles you will be facing. Learn how to reproduce your opponent's techniques. Analyze the strengths and weaknesses of every position you train. Discover how to effectively neutralize and counter their strong movements, and learn how to explore your opponent's weaknesses. Pay a lot of attention to how your adversaries were previously defeated. Start by analyzing how they get points scored against them, which moves, which sides, what circumstance, what submissions they get submitted by in their journey, and what submissions they never get submitted because they always manage to escape. Build an elimination process system where you can build statistics. Based on that analysis you can develop and effective strategy.

Roger Gracie is known famously for winning tournaments back to back with the cross choke from mount. He once was asked how people are still not able to defend such move. He responded that it is because his adversaries train wrong. People ask training partners to do their own version of the cross choke so they can train the defense, but none of them cared to learn how Roger effectively performs the move in its finest details so they can then learn correctly how to defend his cross choke. You must dedicate time and have an open mind to investigate your opponent's strengths and learn how to prevent, neutralize and counter them.

THE BRAZILIAN JIU-JITSU WAY

勇気

"In battle, if you make your opponent flinch, you have already won."

- Miyamoto Musashi

4 – SCORE

A couple of years ago I started noticing that the Jiu-Jitsu practiced in the academy, more recreationally speaking, where there is not much attention paid to time, it is very common that one win by submission overcoming a difficult situation. To give a clear picture here is an example: Two players start sparring and they go over various positions, one sweeps the other, then mounts him, the other one escapes and the one that was mounted still is able to achieve a submission and win later on.

In comparison, I noted that in competitive Jiu-Jitsu in IBJJF tournaments, unlike the recreational Jiu-Jitsu, the person who scored points first, most of the time ended up winning. This is due the short time of combat and the ability and interest in stalling to make the time run out.

I decided to research more deeply into this observation and I documented matches in several divisions from blue to black in IBJJF championships. I found out that in 87% of the cases, the person who scores a point first, decisively won more often.

So is it correct to say that a student should focus on pursuing means to obtain points right away? To focus and specialize in take downs or sweeps? I would say yes!

Some instructors might say that this is a wrong statement as Jiu-Jitsu in the self-defense perspective is also an art that is prime to defend, to counter, to react, etc. Again, I must say that this book is intended to students that would like to engage and succeed in high level competition. I am not talking about self-defense, Jiu-Jitsu for MMA, neither the original Gracie Jiu-Jitsu here, but I must say this to the people that train sport Jiu-Jitsu for self-defense purposes only: Points in Brazilian Jiu-Jitsu are a reward for the achievement of territory gain, for obtaining or advancing dominant positions. In other words, if in a self-defense situation one takes the aggressor's back, he wouldn't get four points for that but most likely a competent practitioner would defeat his opponent. The same applies if you take someone down and land in side control. Similarly if someone takes you down and that moment of disorientation of falling on the concrete with an aggressor on top punching you, is a translation of inferiority that must be dealt with, and hopefully overcome.

仁

"The important thing in strategy is to suppress the enemy's useful actions but allow his useless actions."

- Miyamoto Musashi

5 – GRIPS

Most Jiu-Jitsu students focus mostly in movements at large, for instance, the fashionable sweep of the year, or the last deadly spinning choke hold. Looking at movements at large is not what happens in the high level scene however. At some point in our journey we start to pay attention to black belts fighting at a slow pace, and then we are able to see in action the most important element in this art – grip fighting.

Because many of the characteristics of grip fighting are boring and static, it gives the impression that it is an abstract element of fighting. Grip fighting gives the sense to the spectator of no importance, and to a beginner student, it can be seriously overlooked.

At the beginner level, one can benefit from a deliberate mistake and advance in position, or one can replicate the proper steps of a technique, and if the opponent doesn't react effectively to neutralize or counter it, the move can be successful as well.

In general we are taught to replicate a maneuver by following linear steps: one, two and three, for example, grab here, hook there and lock over there. Students are then introduced to the importance of grips and their correct positioning. I also remind students that if you deliberately change one inch of your grip, without understanding its purpose, the performance of the move could be deteriorated. However, we are all human beings, and as Jiu-Jitsu is very dynamic in terms of body and mind, it is very easy to get side tracked.

There are many factors that can contribute to a student altering the correct grip necessary in a specific situation that can ruin its performance, such as hesitation, fatigue, balance, time left, patience, and many others. But the number one reason of a student to make a move that he shouldn't do, is one hundred percent voluntarily. Countless are the times I've seen a student so close to submitting an opponent and he lets go of that grip. Hundreds of the times I have seen students with a perfect grip controlling the pants of a dangerous guard player specialized in triangles and omoplatas, when in open guard securing the position, being safe, disturbing the opponent's strategy, suddenly and for no reason whatsoever, the student let go of the grip that was the pillar of that moment, only to then get easily submitted immediately after such release.

Proper grips must be learned and exercised mentally as well by one having focus and discipline. An effective grip empowers the player with leverage and confidence, and at the same time disempowering the opponent physically and psychologically. The strength of the correct grip creates a chain reaction in the opponent that begins with the realization of the inability to exercise the movement he had in mind after a few attempts of a specific technique. This advent forces the opponent to regroup and seek adaptation or completely change his plan. Psychologically, this is already the beginning of mental defeat, as usually the fighter is specialized only in certain moves. He may choose a secondary maneuver or variation, still conservative in most cases, in order to continue the wave of attack. If the opponent doesn't succeed on this new bid, another change in his mind will occur: he will switch the mode from being on the offense to the defense. In other words, the survival instinct will start to arise in his mind. High level Jiu-Jitsu players are not conditioned to defend, they are conditioned to attack, to push, to drive, to win. When put in this defensive situation, most athletes make reckless technical choices out of desperation, generated by the frustration caused by the inability to execute his game plan as he is being stopped by an effective grip.

A classic example can be described and experienced by any beginner. The moves necessary for this experience are the cross choke from closed guard and the armbar, also from the guard. Imagine you are inside your training partner's closed guard and you control one of his sleeves or wrist with both of your hands, keeping it away from your neck and away from your legs at the same time. If you ask him to attempt the cross choke, he will try to move his hand towards your neck, you will resist, and he will tell you he can't do it. Now, if you ask him to try an armbar from the guard, you will see several people hesitating in at least trying it. That's because they failed once, so they are being conditioned to anticipate their next move's failure probability. They will know they don't have the proper grip to attempt such move, they feel disempowered, and they feel it is wrong to do so.

If you attempt such a technique during a sparring session, most likely after a minute or so, your opponent will recklessly open the guard to attempt "something". Why do I say the word "something"? Because if you have never been trained to execute in Jiu-Jitsu a maneuver while being "handicapped", such as having one hand dominated by two hands, there should be no reason to open the guard at first place. It is a shot in your own foot. You will be simply giving an easy pass to your opponent. Most of the times you will pass the guard with no technique. You will simply just run over to side control without much resistance.

This is a simple fascinating experiment, easy to understand but yet, most students don't retain such concepts and apply in all other possible positions covered by Jiu-Jitsu.

In sum, no position in high level Jiu-Jitsu can be obtained without proper grips because there are less errors performed by the fighters, with the exception of isolated factors as fatigue, mental defeat, lack of time, etc.

礼

"You must understand that there is more than one path to the top of the mountain."

- Miyamoto Musashi

"So in war, the way is to avoid what is strong, and strike at what is weak."

- Sun Tzu

6 – PATHWAY

Everyone performs moves better on one side than the other. This is a fact. Rare are the practitioners who train every single technique equally on both sides, and even if you do, you would still have your favorite side.

A long time ago I started to notice that some people are not able to pass the guard at all in some fights, while in others they are able to pass and establish side control very quickly. We start to wonder sometimes if the bottom player is too good or too bad and the same goes for the top player that is trying to pass.

In a recent study I started to clock the time spent when a student is trying to pass the guard attacking one side only and later on, on the other side. The result of this analysis was incredible. I was actually able to record footage of a student executing such concepts at the IBJJF Miami International Open in 2011. The interpretation is the following: A student spent 54 seconds trying to pass the half-guard attacking on one side only using a specific technique, and he was not able to accomplish the move. He was actually brought back to full guard after his attempt.

He was trained to recognize the strong "side" of his adversary and to not insist on such an attack after one attempt to the opponents strong side. The rationale in only attacking once is to conserve energy and to be more effective when attacking the other side that is expected to be relatively weaker, as it is a fact that most of practitioners are not equally skilled when performing moves on both sides. The result is that in only 24 seconds of attacking the other side, using the very same technique he used previously, this student was not only able to pass the guard, but he ended up going straight to the mount position, obtaining a total of seven points for this maneuver.

In high-level competition it is important to not waste time and energy with what can generate frustration, poisoning the student's mind with hesitation and lack of confidence, after a failed attempt to perform a technique.

One must enter a match already knowing what the strengths and weaknesses of the adversary are. In many cases when this is not possible, it may be possible to "read" your opponent during the combat. A hand on the ground, a tilt of a knee, the first hand to grab your collar, those are signs among many others that allow you to profile an opponent and immediately create a counter tactical plan to neutralize his strong points and to take advantage of his weaknesses.

THE BRAZILIAN JIU-JITSU WAY

誠

"All warfare is based on deception. Hence, when able to attack, we must seem unable; when using our forces, we must seem inactive; when we are near, we must make the enemy believe we are far away; when far away, we must make him believe we are near."

- Sun Tzu

7 – AMBUSH

Many people talk about the importance of transitions in Jiu-Jitsu, but rarely someone defines transitions beyond the flow drill or even breaks it down. I find it easier to comprehend transitions used in competition in two distinctive ways: the deceptive transition and the powered transition, which will be explained in the following chapter.

The deceptive transition consists of movements that create a chain of techniques where the use of power is extremely low. Such moves stand by the ultimate meaning of deception which is the act to deceive, to give false impression. In Jiu-Jitsu, this manifests by leading your opponent in a direction where he thinks is correct, but in reality it will lead him to defeat.

A classic example of a basic deceptive transition used in the beginner level is the armbar performed from the mount, letting the opponent escape in a rotational move where he falls directly into a triangle. Another typical maneuver is from the inside the guard, when the top player sticks one hand between the legs as he is putting himself into a triangle choke, but due to anticipation he can timely avoid the triangle, passing the guard and advancing to an easy side control.

In modern high level Jiu-Jitsu, the concept is still used in various combinations. The main difference now is that not only is deception used to allow the opponent to naively go for a move that will lead him directly to a loss of territory, but also to generate confusion and hesitation in the mist of the sophisticated fight for points and advantages.

This new perspective is clearly perceived with the advancement of the Dela Riva guard towards double guard and Berimbolo, where the defendant is in check as he doesn't know if his adversary is pursuing the submission, back or simply a sweep. Either way, as the competitor knows that to stay behind the scoreboard by two points can be fatal, the nightmare of the possibility of being behind by four points if the back is taken, generates enormous mental confusion and anxiety which can lead one to commit a premature or inevitable mistake.

These are the light, bright, ghost Jiu-Jitsu tactics that must be applied in high level competition in order to obtain success. Jiu-Jitsu must be played with the mind and the body and not only the body. Competitors should investigate methods of utilizing this concept in many positions, as this can be the difference between an ordinary fighter and a world class one. Be ghost!

THE BRAZILIAN JIU-JITSU WAY

名誉

*"Let your plans be dark
and impenetrable as night,
and when you move,
fall like a thunderbolt."*

- Sun Tzu

8 – ASSAULT

The difference between the two types of transitions defined in this book is the intensity level of power and deception applied towards a combination of moves. Unlike the deceptive transition, which doesn't require the use of power, as it relies on misguiding your opponent into a specific position, I can define powered transition as a chain of techniques that are enforced by the use of power (maximum force in minimum time) in the form of an explosive action of combined movements.

Powered transitions are not to be confused with pushing or dictating the pace of the match, as these will be discussed later in this book.

These power transition types of attacks create disturbance in the opponent's mind as he is assaulted by the use of power in combination with a series of moves. This approach causes a fear of defeat. This must be explored when launching an attack to obtain points, followed by an attempt to advance position or to submit the opponent.

Initial attacks, once successful, can create a short window of opportunity where a winning move can be applied in a certain situation in a tremendously short period of time. This situation I call the "disorienting window of opportunity" and will be discussed in the next chapter.

Some athletes miss such opportunities by advancing position and settling immediately after, without attempting a submission or seeking more points. With the advent of the rule of cumulative points (IBJJF), an athlete should not overlook the possibility to explore such combinations.

A clear picture of powered transitions are easy to exemplify when you see an athlete attempting a take down that fails, and another instant attempt is executed and another one and so on. Many times you see adversaries collapsing just because they are being charged and the attack combinations are coming faster than one can process the correct defensive actions that must be taken.

Here is one of the most classic examples of a powered transition: Refer to the final match of the adult black belt division of the 2012 IBJJF World Championship, where Marcus Almeida in the last nine seconds of the ten minute match is losing by two points and takes Leonardo Nogueira down to score two points, tying the match and in the very last second mounting his opponent, winning the Absolute World Championship by one advantage (awarded after the match has ended), in the last second.

Investigate the psychological value of executing powered transitions. Research and practice techniques that connect well to each other that are part of your game. Use this concept to train your defenses as well as it will give you better understanding of the nightmare your opponent will be facing.

For instance, the difference between an ordinary armbar from a devastating explosive end-of-match armbar is in the pre-stage of the performance of the armbar per-se. One can practice the armbar in the dojo as fast as they can and they can do the same armbar with the same speed in a tournament. However the optic and the effect of the same move will be perceived differently if one comes from a static or settled position and the other comes from the immediate advancement from a previous position.

Use strength and speed when transitioning to force you opponent to succumb. Fall like a thunderbolt.

"When you decide to attack, keep calm and dash in quickly, forestalling the enemy... attack with a feeling of constantly crushing the enemy, from first to last."

- Miyamoto Musashi

9 – OPPORTUNITY

While studying black belt matches in IBJJF tournaments, specifically submission occurrences, one thing caught my attention: There are very few competitors that effectively defended against attacks in which such maneuvers allowed an athlete to escape from a submission hold. What actually caught my attention was the fact that many athletes do not even initiate any attempt to defend – they simply give up.

Reflecting upon this situation I started to think of several hypotheses that may apply to the perfect execution of a technique that may cause instant injury, or in other words, the competence and merit of the attacker. I also thought about what really causes mental defeat, the quitting thoughts, the giving up, to not even try to defend, to escape. In the dojo, when a higher rank applies a submission hold in a lower rank student, many times this student gives up as he is mentally defeated as he knows there is no point in resisting such attack which could aggravate his condition and could cause injury and ultimately the waste of energy. In the dojo, nobody is competing as in a tournament set.

Let's understand that in high level competition there is no such "respect" among athletes. Nobody will give up because someone's rank, last name or titles. A well-prepared competitor doesn't have such thoughts crossing his mind. He is there to fight anyone and he is there to win. The ones who do not have such mindset do not climb to the top of the mountain. I would like to emphasize once again that I am talking about competitors of high level. Those are the guys that in a bracket of 100 people make to the top 4 every single tournament and they absolutely shine when they become black belts.

So, by understanding how the defeated player's mind functions, and knowing that those guys are not there to "participate" only, let's analyze now what contributes to the attacker succeeding in submitting other high level competitors.

The answer for this examination in my perspective is timing. By reflecting upon matches where fast submissions occurred, I noticed that fast transitions resulted in indefensible submission holds. This concept happens lots of times after a devastating throw followed by a speedy armbar, for instance, or the athlete that jumps guard and successfully applies an armbar or when pulling guard magically locks a triangle choke. Sometimes it looks so easy that is unbelievable. Why? The answer is because they are caused by a delay of reaction time that is a consequence of failure in preventing and countering the first move performed by the adversary that resulted in a sort of mental or physical impact.

A successful competitor cannot philosophize about what his adversary is doing or will do. Such hesitating reasoning freezes his ability to attack, to put pressure, to drive. An athlete is conditioned to process more information about himself and less in regards to the opponent's movements. I am not saying one should disregard what the adversary is doing. I am saying that an athlete is conditioned to be confident and push his game, and therefore he spends more energy thinking about what he is doing and what he will do rather than thinking what can happen if he does this or that, or what will happen if the opponent does this or that. A competitor is conditioned to just do it and find out the outcome afterward.

In this sphere, there is little time to perform fast transitions and I call it a "disorienting window of opportunity". This is the moment where for example your adversary is either surprised by a move of impact (such a hip throw) or because of the realization of losing a certain position that he was employing mental and physical energy to defend at all costs. This is why you see athletes for instance performing a hip throw followed by an instant armbar, or when an athlete finally frees his leg from half-guard moving towards side control and he immediately performs a quick armbar. In such situation you will not see the defendant attempt any resistance, he simply taps out.

The "disorienting window opportunity" must be further investigated by the athlete so he can learn how to condition the mind to foresee the moment and prepare the body to execute a move that fits the situation, which can reduce to the lowest levels the opponent's ability to defend and escape from a devastating attack.

"Thus the expert in battle moves the enemy, and is not moved by him."

- Sun Tzu

"If you do not control the enemy, the enemy will control you."

- Miyamoto Musashi

10 – HEART

At the end of the day the one who has the strongest desire to win, in most cases is the most accomplished competitor.

During the preparation of one's career, drive and readiness can ensure that everything that could be done for the most important moment of the athlete's season has been accomplished. After the match starts, another element plays the most important role in the athlete's mind in order to ensure discipline, determination, focus and perseverance, so that tactics and strategies are properly executed in the most adverse situations: This element is called will.

Will is also known in sports as 'heart". The one who has the "biggest heart" is the one who will most likely win.

As for instance, the ability to overcome difficult situations such as reversing a scoreboard when he is behind, or to run against time and against a stalling opponent, only he who has more "heart" will be capable to complete such task.

Having heart also ensures that the pace of the match can be dictated from beginning to end and in most of the cases, when one starts the match scoring points first, it is very unlikely that he will lose control of his opponent.

Dominance in the form of control can only be achieved with a large amount of focus fueled by the desire to win, the desire to crush, to not give space, to not give your opponent a single chance.

When winning, time runs in your opponent's mind like poison and increases the level of frustration by dominating the match at all times, fatally leads the opponent to commit a mistake caused by mental defeat. Too many mistakes altogether are the cause for an adversary to give up and succumb.

Make sure to make your opponent play your game and do not play his game. This way you neutralize his strategy. If you see yourself playing your opponent's game, you must take action immediately. Apply the previously studied methods to neutralize his best maneuvers and change the position as soon as possible. Avoid this scenario at all costs. This can be achieved by leading the scoreboard first, dictating the pace, and using time against your opponent.

When the time 'heart' comes to play has arrived, it means you are living the center, the peak of the entire training season. Enter the match knowing you dedicated one hundred percent of everything you could have done to prepare yourself. This will give you the necessary confidence that will make you feel invincible. The feeling that you really deserve the first place and you are there to fight for what belongs to you.

Heart is the end of the training cycle presented in this piece that is repeated in every competition season. Be sure that if you have the drive and have put in every possible effort to get ready, the fire that is within you will certainly be unleashed during your performances, bringing many victories in your journey.

THE BRAZILIAN JIU-JITSU WAY

忠義

ABOUT THE AUTHOR

Professor Thadeu Vieira is a native of Rio de Janeiro. He is a third degree black belt and graduated with his degree in Physical Education from the University of Volta Redonda (UNIFOA) in Rio de Janeiro State. In 2002, Master Paulo Wesley Lopes (Student of Grand Master Francisco Mansor ← Grand Master Helio Gracie) awarded Professor Vieira with his black belt in Brazilian Jiu-Jitsu. Professor Vieira has specialized in teaching Brazilian Jiu-Jitsu to children, and he has several students that have been awarded gold medals in the Brazilian National, Florida State, Pan American and World Championships, in all ages. He currently lives in Sarasota, Florida, where he has established the headquarters of his competition team, the Vieira Jiu-Jitsu Association.

ACKNOWLEDGMENTS

I would like to thank all my students that throughout the years allowed me the privilege of teaching them. In every hour we spent together, you taught me how to become a better teacher and I sincerely thank you all for that.